FIRST PEOPLES

THE AYMARA

OF SOUTH AMERICA

JAMES EAGEN

Lerner Publications Company • Minneapolis

**First American edition published in 2002
by Lerner Publications Company**

Published by arrangement with Times Editions
Copyright © 2002 by Times Media Private Limited

Lerner Publications Company
A division of Lerner Publishing Group
241 First Avenue North
Minneapolis, MN 55401 U.S.A.
Website address: www.lernerbooks.com

Series originated and designed by
Times Editions
An imprint of Times Media Private Limited
A member of the Times Publishing Group
1 New Industrial Road, Singapore 536196
Website address: www.timesone.com.sg/te

Series editors: Margaret J. Goldstein, Oh Hwee Yen
Series designers: Tuck Loong, Loo Chuan Ming
Series picture researcher: Susan Jane Manuel

Library of Congress Cataloging-in-Publication Data
Eagen, James.
The Aymara of South America / by James Eagen.— 1st American ed.
p. cm. -- (First peoples)
Includes bibliographical references and index.
Summary: Describes the history, culture, economy, geographic location, and
religion of the Aymara people of South America's high plains, featuring their
struggle to obtain equal rights and to maintain their cultural heritage.
ISBN 0-8225-4174-2 (lib. bdg. : alk. paper)
1. Aymara Indians--Juvenile literature. [1. Aymara Indians.
2. Indians of South America] I. Title. II. Series.
F2230.2.A9 E24 2002
980'.00498324—dc21   2001004235

Printed in Malaysia
Bound in the United States of America

1 2 3 4 5 6—0S—07 06 05 04 03 02

CONTENTS

WHO ARE THE AYMARA?

The Aymara are Indian people who live in the South American countries of Argentina, Bolivia, Chile, Ecuador, and Peru. In total, more than 2 million Aymara live in South America. About half of them live around Lake Titicaca, which lies at the border of Peru and Bolivia. The Aymara are divided into smaller groups, including the Canchi, Caranga, Charca, Colla, Collagua, Collahuaya, Lupaca, Omasuyo, Pacasa, Quillaca, and Ubina. These groups share a common language, also called Aymara. The Aymara live alongside other Indian people, such as the Chipaya and the Quechua.

Keeping Their Culture Alive

For more than ten thousand years, the Aymara have kept their traditional ways. They continue to speak their old language, along with Spanish. They still farm, herd, and fish for a living like their ancestors did. But they have also adapted to modern ways. While most Aymara live in the countryside, some live in big cities such as La Paz, Bolivia. Urban areas provide more jobs and schools than rural areas do. Many young Aymara people attend college in big cities.

AYMARA AND FOREIGNERS

The Aymara (*right*) have fought many wars with foreign people who have invaded their land. These people include the Inca, a powerful Indian group who conquered the Aymara in the mid-1400s, and the Spanish, who defeated the Inca one century later. Because outsiders have invaded Aymara lands, the Aymara sometimes distrust foreigners. Some Aymara believe in supernatural beings with white faces, jackets, leather boots, and wide-brimmed hats. These beings are said to attack Aymara communities. The belief probably began with the fear of the Spanish, who enslaved the Aymara and took away their land. Although the Aymara might be suspicious at first, once outsiders win their trust, they will find that the Aymara are friendly and helpful.

AMONG THE SKIES

Most Aymara live on the Altiplano, which means "high plain." It is a plateau (raised, flat, and level land) that stretches from southern Peru down to the southwestern corner of Bolivia. It measures around 600 miles (965 kilometers) long and 80 miles (129 kilometers) wide. The Altiplano sits at an approximate height of 12,000 feet (3,658 meters) above sea level. Tall mountain ranges surround the Altiplano—the Cordillera Occidental to the west and the Cordillera Real to the east. These ranges are part of the Andes Mountains, a vast South American mountain chain.

Below: The dry landscape of the Altiplano. Less than 5 inches (12.7 centimeters) of rain falls on the Altiplano each year.

Altiplano Weather

The Altiplano is a cold region. The average daily temperature is only about 45 degrees Fahrenheit (7 degrees Celsius). However, temperatures can sometimes reach as high as 90 degrees Fahrenheit (32 degrees Celsius) and as low as 10 degrees Fahrenheit (-12 degrees Celsius). The Altiplano has only two seasons. The dry season lasts from May to November. The rainy season starts in December and ends in April.

Lake Titicaca

Lake Titicaca is one of the many lakes on the Altiplano. It is located in the middle of the Altiplano. At 12,500 feet (3,810 meters) above sea level, Lake Titicaca is one of the highest lakes in the world. It is also the second largest lake in South America. It covers more than 3,200 square miles (8,288 square kilometers). More than twenty-five rivers drain into Lake Titicaca.

Above: Two ways to sail on Lake Titicaca: in traditional reed boats or motor-powered ones

Snow-Covered Peaks

Snow-covered mountains surround the Altiplano. The tallest mountain is Mount Sajama, located in the Cordillera Occidental. It reaches 21,463 feet (6,542 meters) above sea level. Mount Illimani, which is located in the Cordillera Real, also rises above 21,000 feet (6,400 meters). Illimani has five peaks that tower over the city of La Paz, Bolivia.

Above: Snow covers the peaks of the Cordillera Real. Many of the mountains surrounding the Altiplano are actually active volcanoes.

INTO THIN AIR

The amount of oxygen in the air decreases with altitude, or height above sea level. To get enough oxygen at high altitudes, people must breathe very hard. However, a person can get used to the decreased oxygen levels over time. Over many generations, the Aymara have adjusted to the low oxygen levels in the great heights of the Altiplano. They have bigger lungs than people who dwell closer to sea level. They have more red blood cells, which help their bodies absorb more oxygen.

ALTIPLANO VEGETATION

The plants on the Altiplano have adapted to the cold, dry environment. Some of the plants have hollow stems that can store extra water for use in the dry season. Some plants have roots that grow close to the surface of the ground. When it rains, the shallow roots can absorb rainwater quickly. Other plants have thick leaves or thick bark that acts like a winter coat. This "coat" traps heat in the plant and helps keep the water inside the plant from freezing.

Below: Two Aymara boys having fun swimming among the totora reeds

Above: This strange-looking plant is a clump of yareta moss, one of the hardy plants that survive on the Altiplano.

Plants and Trees

Shrubs, tall grasses, and mosses are common on the Altiplano. Dandelions and eucalyptus trees thrive there. Kara plants are tall, with broad leaves and sharp spines. They can grow in just a thin crust of soil on steep rocky slopes. Tall thin reeds known as totoras grow near the shores of Lake Titicaca.

Useful Plants

The Aymara grow some plants for food, including potatoes, maize (corn), barley, beans, and onions. Some Aymara crops are unfamiliar to most people in North America and Europe. Examples include quinoa, a grain that's rich in protein and minerals, and oca, a sour root that's high in carbohydrates.

ONCE IN A HUNDRED YEARS

Puya raimondii (*right*), a relative of the pineapple, grows only on the Altiplano. It can grow to be 6 feet (1.8 meters) tall. At about one hundred years old, the plant bursts into white flowers. After flowering, the plant slowly dies.

ANIMALS FRIENDLY AND FIERCE

The Aymara could not survive without their animals. Animals provide meat for food and wool for clothes. They also carry heavy loads. Thousands of years ago, the Aymara domesticated (tamed) the alpaca, llama, dog, and guinea pig. The Spanish brought other domesticated animals to Aymara lands in the 1500s. These animals included chickens, cows, donkeys, ducks, geese, horses, pigs, and sheep.

Wild Animals

Many wild animals live in the Altiplano, including wolves, foxes, deer, and rodents. Guanacos are wild cousins of the llama. Guanacos have small heads and long legs. The majestic Andean condor soars above the Altiplano. This bird has a wingspan of over 10 feet (3 meters). It is one of the world's largest birds of prey.

Above: Viscachas may look like rabbits but are actually wild rodents that live in the Altiplano.

Below: Donkeys help Aymara farmers carry the harvest.

Alpacas and Llamas

Alpacas and llamas are South American mammals that are related to camels. Alpacas and llamas have small heads, large pointed ears, and long necks and legs. They also have large padded feet, which are ideal for walking on stony ground in the mountains. On average, llamas weigh 300 pounds (136 kilograms), and alpacas weigh 150 pounds (68 kilograms). The alpaca and llama are very useful to the Aymara. They carry heavy loads and provide people with meat and wool. Their dung is good fertilizer for the soil. The Aymara have raised alpacas and llamas for more than five thousand years.

Above: Llamas have split upper lips that allow them to pluck leaves from thorny plants. Llamas also have more red blood cells than animals that live close to sea level. These cells help llamas absorb more oxygen in the high Altiplano environment.

Animals of the Lake

Beautiful Lake Titicaca is full of fish, including catfish, trout, and pejerry—a kind of mackerel. Ispi are small silvery fish measuring up to 3.5 inches (9 centimeters) long. Killifish are equally small fish with black stripes. The Aymara eat lots of fish from the lake and sell extra fish at markets. The lake is also home to ducks, geese, and some unusual reptiles. One example is the telmatobius, a giant frog measuring 12 inches (30 centimeters) long.

SACRED ANIMALS

The Aymara believe that some animals, such as the alpaca, condor, fox, llama, and sheep, have supernatural powers. These animals are considered sacred. The Aymara often weave images of these sacred animals into textiles (*right*). They also sacrifice (kill) certain animals, such as llamas, to show respect to the gods.

ANCESTORS OF THE AYMARA

Scientists believe that the ancestors of the Aymara crossed into the Americas from Asia between 60,000 and 20,000 years ago. They probably walked across a strip of land that once connected eastern Siberia and Alaska. The people moved southward, eventually reaching South America around 11,000 years ago.

Above: The Puerta del Sol, or the Gateway of the Sun, one of the stone structures in Tiahuanaco

From Nomads to Farmers

The early Aymara were nomads. They traveled from place to place, without permanent homes. From the Altiplano, the Aymara sometimes ventured to the coasts of Chile and Peru, where they fished in the Pacific Ocean. Sometime after 4000 B.C., the Aymara started to grow crops around Lake Titicaca. Because they had to look after their farms, the Aymara could not travel as much as they had before. So, they settled down around the lake.

The Sacred City

By A.D. 600, about 20,000 people from different groups were living on the Altiplano. The groups included the Aymara, Chipaya, Pukina, and Uru. These people built a vast city, Tiahuanaco, on the southern shore of Lake Titicaca in present-day Bolivia. Some archaeologists (scientists who study the remains of past cultures) believe that the city might have covered more than 4 square miles (10 square kilometers).

A Ghost Town

Between A.D. 1000 and 1100, Tiahuanaco was abandoned. Scientists aren't sure why, because the inhabitants did not keep written records. According to one theory, a drought occurred on the Altiplano from A.D. 900 to 1400. People living in Tiahuanaco probably left the city for surrounding valleys that had more water.

Above: Tiahuanaco might have been abandoned because of a drought.

MOVING STONES

Tiahuanaco (*left*) held pyramids, temples, and other stone structures. These structures were made of huge slabs of andesite (a black volcanic rock) and sandstone. The sandstone probably came from a quarry 6 miles (9.6 kilometers) from the city. However, the nearest andesite quarry lies 62 miles (100 kilometers) from Tiahuanaco. This fact poses a big question: How did the Aymara get the andesite to Tiahuanaco? According to Aymara lore, the gods commanded the stones to move, and they tumbled into place. However, archaeologists think the ancient builders floated the stones across Lake Titicaca on reed boats.

THE PEOPLE OF THE SUN

O f all the Indian groups living in the Andes, the Inca were the most powerful. They built a vast empire along the western coast of South America, including parts of Argentina, Bolivia, Chile, Ecuador, and Peru.

Left: An Inca Indian. The Inca were known as "the People of the Sun" because they worshiped Viracocha, the Sun God. The Inca believed he created all human beings.

Inca Conquerors

In the mid-1400s, the Inca conquered the Aymara and other groups living around Lake Titicaca. The Inca were skilled warriors. They fought with spears, slingshots, darts, and clubs. They protected their bodies with quilted cloth, helmets, and shields. The Aymara and other Indian groups were not well-trained warriors. They did not wear protective armor. The Inca easily defeated them.

Right: An Inca king with his servants. Although they were fearsome warriors, the Inca were good rulers. They believed that a king showed his wealth and power by being generous toward his subjects.

Life under the Inca

Inca rulers taxed the Aymara and other conquered groups. The Aymara were also forced to work for the Inca, practice the Inca religion, and speak Quechua, the language of the Inca. Nevertheless, life for the Aymara and other groups did not change very much under Inca rule. The conquered Indians continued to farm, just as they had before the Inca arrived. On the whole, the Inca were good rulers. Inca kings were generous and helped the conquered people with gifts of food and money.

THE PAST LIVES ON

The Inca influence lives on in the Andes region. Old Inca shrines, temples, and the ruins of ancient Inca architecture (*left*) still stand in the mountains near La Paz. People still use roads built by the Incas hundreds of years ago. The modern Aymara religion also contains elements of the old Inca religion.

THE SPANISH INVASION

In the 1500s, Spanish conquerors arrived in Central and South America, searching for gold, silver, and other riches. In 1532 they came to the Altiplano. Through bloody battles, the Spanish took over the land and the people, including the Inca, the Aymara, and other Indian groups.

Rulers from Europe

The king of Spain sent governors, soldiers, and settlers to South America. The Spanish set up new colonies, passed new laws, and collected taxes from the Aymara and other Indians. Catholic priests also came to South America from Spain. They convinced many Aymara to adopt the Catholic faith.

Below: The native Indians fought bravely against the Spanish. But their spears, stone clubs, and slingshots were no match for the Spaniards' cannons, guns, and swords.

Above: The Spanish conquerors were cruel to the Indians. Here, they burn an Inca chief.

New Landowners

The Spanish took over the Indians' farms. They built haciendas, or large plantations, there. They enslaved the Indians and forced them to work on the haciendas as farmers, watchmen, shepherds, cooks, and other household servants. In exchange for their labor, Indians received small plots of land, where they could grow some crops for their families.

Difficult Work, Difficult Times

In 1545 the Spanish discovered silver in western Bolivia, south of Lake Titicaca. The Spaniards built silver mines and exported the silver to Spain, where it was made into coins and other objects. The Spanish mine owners became wealthy, but the Aymara and other Indians suffered during this period. Spanish rulers forced many Indian men to work in the mines. The miners, called *mitayos*, worked twelve-hour shifts. They stayed underground for up to four months at a time. The work was dangerous. Mines often collapsed, and falling rocks injured or killed many miners. Many miners fell sick from exposure to mercury, a poisonous metal used to process silver.

POTOSÍ

Potosí, Bolivia, was once the largest city in the Americas. During the 1670s, as many as 200,000 people lived there. Potosí was a big silver mining center, producing more silver than any other place in the world. The mines (*right*) were so big that the Indian people could not provide enough labor. The Spanish had to bring in African slaves to work in the mines.

THE FIGHT FOR LIBERATION

Spain ruled Bolivia, Argentina, Chile, Ecuador, Peru, and other South American countries for many years. Eventually, many people in South America grew unhappy with Spanish rule and started to fight for independence from Spain. These people included Indians such as the Aymara, Spanish people born in South America, colonists from other European countries, African slaves, and people of mixed race. After many violent struggles, most South American nations gained independence in the 1800s.

The Struggle to Be Free

In 1781, an Aymara man named Tupac Katari led a group of Indian men in a riot in La Paz. The rioters were angry because Spanish rulers had raised their taxes. For seven months, Katari and his group attacked the Spanish. The Indians destroyed many Spanish churches and government buildings. In the 1800s, Argentinean general José de San Martin led the fight for independence. Under his leadership, Argentina won independence in 1816, and Chile won independence in 1818. Around the same time, General Simón Bolívar, a Venezuelan soldier, helped win independence for Bolivia, Venezuela, Colombia, Ecuador, and Peru.

Left: A statue of General Simón Bolívar in La Paz

Life after Independence

Although Spain had been defeated, life was still difficult for the Aymara. People of Spanish heritage still owned most of the land and the silver mines in South America. The Aymara and other Indians still had to work for the wealthy landowners and mine owners. Their wages were low, and working conditions were poor.

Above: Miners and their supporters march on the streets of Potosí.

Taking Back the Land

For many years, the Aymara and other Indians complained about low pay and dangerous working conditions in the mines. But the mine owners did not make improvements. Finally, in the mid-1950s, the frustrated mitayos fought back with armed strikes and protests. They used force to take over the mines for themselves. Around the same time, Indian people fought to take back the haciendas from the Spanish. In Bolivia, the Indians were successful in this fight. In other countries, the Aymara and other Indians are still fighting for control of their ancient homelands.

AYMARA IN POWER

In the late 1900s, Aymara leaders started to play important roles in local and national politics. These leaders included Felipe Quispe (*right*), Hugo Cárdenas, and Gregorio Ticona Gomez. Quispe fought for the rights of Aymara people in Bolivia. Cárdenas served as vice president of Bolivia from 1993 to 1998. In 1998, Gomez became the mayor of Puno, Peru.

WEALTH OF THE LAND

Like their ancestors, present-day Aymara fish, farm, and herd animals for a living. Herders roam the grasslands of the Altiplano with packs of alpacas and llamas. Farmers and fishermen work around Lake Titicaca. Farmers prepare their fields and sow seeds between August and November. They harvest crops from late March to May. Fishing and herding are year-round activities.

Farming the Land

The Aymara grow quinoa, potatoes, maize, barley, beans, and onions on their farms. Potatoes are the main crop, and the Aymara grow two varieties—sweet and bitter. Because the Altiplano is so dry, farmers must irrigate (bring water to) the land. They dig canals to carry water from nearby rivers to their farms. They sometimes plant crops on terraces, steplike ridges cut into the sides of the mountains. It's easier to grow crops on flat terraces than on the rocky mountain slopes. Farmers also grow crops on mounds of soil along the swampy shores of Lake Titicaca.

Right: Aymara farmers use simple, traditional tools such as hoes. But sometimes they use computers to keep track of crop sales and tractors to plow fields.

Fishing for a Living

The Aymara fish with simple nets, lines, hooks, and reed boats. Catfish, pejerry, ispi, and trout are the usual targets because of their delicious taste. In the late afternoon, fishermen lay their nets in the shallow waters near the shores of Lake Titicaca. They collect their catches from the nets the next morning.

Above: Aymara women lay out the catch of the day on reed mats.

The Work of the Herders

The Aymara also make a living by herding alpacas and llamas. The typical herd has twelve to fifteen animals. Herding is a full-time job. Herders must trim animals' hooves and check their wool for lice. They have to look out for signs of foot rot, an infection of the hooves. Herders shear alpacas and llamas (trim their fleece, or wool) one to three times a year. They use anything with a sharp edge—knives, pieces of tin, or broken glass—to cut the fleece. The fleece will later be made into soft, warm clothing. The Aymara also use llamas and alpacas as pack animals. Sometimes, young animals are slaughtered for their meat.

THE BARTER ECONOMY

The Aymara have practiced barter, the exchange of goods for other goods, since 4000 B.C. Even in modern times, Aymara farmers exchange crops such as potatoes, oca, and barley for fresh and dried fish, llama meat, and alpaca wool. In city markets, the Aymara trade farm goods for manufactured products like soft drinks, toothpaste, and batteries (*right*).

TOURISM AND THE NEW ECONOMY

Many tourists visit the countries where the Aymara live. The tourists want to see the rain forests, majestic mountains, and warm beaches of Bolivia, Chile, and Peru. Many Aymara have jobs in the tourist industry. They work in hotels and restaurants. There, they meet tourists from the United States, Japan, Europe, and other places. Some visitors want to learn about the Aymara and their unique culture. Many tourists visit Lake Titicaca and the Aymara villages that surround it.

Above: An Aymara textile trader and her wares in a market in Puno, Peru

Right: A tourist visits an Aymara textile store.

Art for Sale

The Aymara used to make textiles and clothes just for their own use. In modern times, the Aymara also sell these products to tourists. People around the world love the Aymara's colorful woven textiles and clothing made from soft and silky alpaca wool. In the cities, tourists crowd into markets to buy Aymara scarves, hats, and gloves. These products are also exported to stores in Europe and North America.

The High Andes and High Adventure

The mountains around the Altiplano are a favorite with mountain climbers from around the world. Aymara guides often lead tours through the mountains. Local herders also rent their llamas to the adventurers. The animals help carry belongings and sometimes even carry the adventurers themselves.

Angels, Llamas, and Cell Phones

The Aymara make small clay figurines that look like angels, llamas, frogs, and other animals and objects. Some figurines represent Pachamama, or Mother Earth. The Aymara even make figurines that look like trucks and cell phones. During religious festivals, the Aymara offer these figurines to Ekeko, the God of Abundance. They hope he will change the miniature objects into the real things. The Aymara also sell these figurines to tourists.

ANCIENT SCULPTURES

Visitors to the Altiplano can see gigantic stone sculptures (*right*). Many were probably built between 300 and 700 years ago. Archaeologists think the Aymara built these sculptures to please their gods and spirits. The Yaya-Mama pillars are well-known Aymara sculptures located near Lake Titicaca. The pillars are decorated with images of plants, people, and two-headed snakes. Nobody knows how many sculptures the Aymara originally made because the Inca and the Spanish destroyed many of them.

HOUSE AND HOME

Hundreds of Aymara villages are located around Lake Titicaca in Bolivia and Peru. About five hundred to one thousand people live in each village. Some areas, such as northern Chile, have fewer Aymara people, with just a few Aymara families living near one another. Each Aymara village usually has its own school and church.

Below: The thick walls of the adobe home slow down heat loss. Therefore, people in adobe houses remain warm throughout the cold Altiplano nights.

What Is Adobe?

Most Aymara homes are built from a material called adobe. Adobe is a mixture of clay, sun-dried earth, sand, and straw. The Aymara sometimes strengthen the mixture with cement. Adobe is a good building material in areas with huge temperature swings. Adobe homes stay warm in cold weather and cool during hot weather.

Homes Made of Earth

The traditional Aymara home was about 8 by 10 feet (2.5 by 3 meters) in size. It had one room and a roof made of turf—a mat of grass, soil, and roots. People slept on animal skins on a platform made of dried mud. The homes did not have electricity or running water. People used candles or oil lamps to light the houses at night. They gathered water from wells, rivers, and lakes. Women cooked meals over an open fire, using eucalyptus wood as fuel.

Left: Aymara children draw water from the village well.

Modern Homes on the Altiplano

Many Aymara people still live in adobe homes. But some live in modern-style houses made of metal, brick, and concrete. Modern Aymara homes often have two rooms. Families sleep on modern-style beds. In big cities, many Aymara have television sets, radios, and plumbing systems in their homes.

Above: An Aymara family in a modern adobe home on the Altiplano

ADOBE FOR EVERYONE

The Aymara are not the only people who build adobe homes. You can also see adobe homes in the deserts of Africa, the mountains of Tibet, and even in the United States. In fact, all the homes and office buildings in Santa Fe, New Mexico, must be built in the adobe style. This is the law!

LIVING AT HOME

The Aymara have large families, with as many as five children, or more, in each. After they get married, children leave home to start their own families. Married sons often build their homes next to their parents' houses. Brothers sometimes live together in one house, along with their wives and children.

Family Education

At a very young age—often by age five—Aymara children learn how to herd animals. Boys are usually in charge of herding, but girls will help out if needed. Girls also learn to harvest potatoes, weave, cook, and take care of their younger siblings. Aymara children also learn about magic, herbal medicine, and religion.

Right: Smile! An Aymara family poses for the camera.

Above: An Aymara boy watches a bird among the reeds of Lake Titicaca.

House Rules

The Aymara father is the head of the family. At home, children must follow the rules that the father lays down. But sons have some rights that fathers do not have. For example, when a son grows up and has his own family, he may visit his father's house and borrow anything he wishes without asking permission. But a father cannot do the same thing in his son's home.

Right: Like most children all over the world, Aymara children have to help out with the housework. This Aymara girl is helping her mother with the washing.

CHILDHOOD FRIENDS

The saying "birds of a feather flock together" means that people who have a lot in common often become good friends. Aymara children might say that "birds of a feather *herd* together." That's because Aymara children often have lots of fun together herding animals. Children who herd together will be friends for years to come.

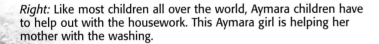

MEN IN THE COMMUNITY

When it comes to farming the land, Aymara men and women are equally important. Men and women work side by side, tilling the soil, sowing seeds, and harvesting crops. However, certain jobs in the Aymara community are open only to men. For instance, only men can work as law enforcers and sorcerers.

Law Enforcers

Jilakatas are the leaders in Aymara communities. They are men who settle disputes and collect taxes. In due time, a jilakata might become a *sot'a,* the most important man in the village. The sot'a is like a sheriff. He makes sure that everyone follows the law.

Right: Aymara men thresh barley on the Altiplano.

Wise Men

Aymara wise men, or sorcerers, are treated with the greatest respect. Called *maestros,* these men are thought to have special powers. The powers come from male gods, so women are not allowed to become maestros. Some maestros say that they have been struck by lightning—a sign that the spirits have singled them out for the job. The Aymara believe that the maestros' skillful magic and wisdom can bring rain to the crops or send dangerous hail far away over the mountains.

Above: An Aymara maestro, surrounded by the village chiefs, chants his prayers to the gods.

Sponsors

Sponsors are men who collect money from the villagers during religious festivals. The money is used for community projects, such as repairing government buildings or installing new water systems. Men take turns being sponsors at different festivals. A man's status in the Aymara community depends on the number of times he has been a sponsor.

JACK OF ALL TRADES

Maestros also work as doctors and healers in the Aymara community. They deliver babies. They make medicines and potions from herbs, bark, and roots. For instance, they boil thistle bark to make a salve for pain. They use dried dandelion roots to help wounds heal. Maestros often travel long distances to gather the plants they need to make medicines.

JOBS FOR WOMEN

Women hold many jobs in the Aymara community. They help tend crops, along with the men. They care for the home, cook meals, and look after the children. Aymara women are also in charge of selling crops at city markets. They travel to the city in trucks with sacks full of potatoes, ocas, and quinoa.

Above: An Aymara woman carries her child on her back.

Right: Aymara women are usually responsible for selling crops at markets. They are also in charge of buying groceries and seeds for planting in their families' farms.

Aymara Specialties

The crops on the farm provide most of the ingredients Aymara women need to make meals. These crops include maize, potatoes, and beans. Aymara families usually eat two meals each day: breakfast and dinner.

Some common Aymara dishes are boiled or steamed sweet potatoes and *chaque de quinoa*, a soup containing quinoa and potatoes. *Humintas* are another traditional Aymara favorite. These are cakes made from crushed maize and sheep's milk cheese, wrapped in the leaves of the maize plant and served baked or boiled. The Aymara also eat fish from Lake Titicaca. One of their favorite dishes is fried ispi, usually eaten with potatoes.

Above: An Aymara woman peeling potatoes for her family's meal

The Maestro's Assistant

Although Aymara women cannot be maestros, they often help maestros prepare herbs and magic potions. They mix the herbs according to the maestro's instructions and pack them for sale. Because of this work, many women know as much as maestros do about herbal cures and magic charms.

PRESERVED POTATOES

The Aymara do not waste anything they grow. They often preserve food for future use. *Chuño,* or freeze-dried potatoes, is one example. To make chuño, the Aymara leave potatoes outside to dry and freeze in the cold mountain air. Then they trample on the potatoes to squeeze out the remaining moisture. After that, they expose the potatoes to the cold, dry air of the Altiplano once more.

DRESSING AYMARA STYLE

Aymara men sometimes wear traditional outfits and sometimes wear modern-style clothing. Aymara women, on the other hand, always wear traditional clothing. Even Aymara women who live in big cities do not wear modern-style outfits.

Above: The Aymara wear sandals and shoes made out of cowhide.

Accessorizing

Aymara women carry all sorts of items—including firewood, crops, and babies—in *ahuayos.* These are hand-woven pieces of cloth measuring about 4 feet by 4 feet (1.2 meters by 1.2 meters). Women sling ahuayos over their backs and tie the ends of the cloth around their necks. Women also wear thick belts woven from llama fleece and human hair.

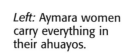

Left: Aymara women carry everything in their ahuayos.

Clothing for Men

Traditional men's attire includes short jackets and bell-bottomed pants with slits at the ankles. To keep warm, men cover themselves with ponchos and *chullos,* woolen caps with earflaps. The wool over the ears is so thick that wearers often cannot hear clearly. An unmarried Aymara man will usually wear a red chullo with a thick white stripe. He will wear a red chullo without a white stripe after he gets married.

Right: These Aymara men wear ponchos to keep warm.

Women's Dress

The most well-known part of the Aymara woman's outfit is a dark green, black, or brown bowler hat. It looks something like an English policeman's hat. Women also wear short blouses and woolen skirts called *polleras.* The skirts are usually red, orange, or blue. Women often wear all the polleras they own wherever they go— sometimes as many as ten at once! Polleras are a sign of wealth, and wealthier women wear more polleras than poor women. Women also wear woolen shawls over their shoulders.

Left: An Aymara woman (*right*) buying salt from an Aymara trader. Aymara women almost always dress in their traditional outfits. But Aymara men, like the salt seller (*left*), often choose to wear Western-style clothing.

AYMARA HAIRSTYLES

Unmarried Aymara women sometimes cut their hair short. They let it grow long after marriage. They part it in the middle and tie it into two long braids. Aymara men usually wear their hair short.

MUSIC AND DANCE

Through songs and dances, the Aymara act out the important events in their history and celebrate their traditional way of life. Old songs and dances are popular, but the Aymara also like modern music, including brass bands and pop music.

Traditional Instruments

Most Aymara men can play one or more traditional wind instruments. The *zampoña* is a kind of panpipe made of reeds. The *sikuri* is a double wind instrument, played by two different musicians at once. Aymara musicians perform at festivals, on city streets, and in city cafés. In the early 1600s, after the Spanish arrived in South America, the Aymara began to make stringed instruments. They copied the design of the Spanish guitar to make a ten-stringed instrument called a *charango.* They used an armadillo shell to make the sound box. In modern times, the Aymara make charangos from wood, not armadillo shells.

Left: A traditional charango made using an armadillo shell (*top*) and a present-day charango made from wood (*bottom*)

Left: An Aymara musician playing a zampoña

Aymara Dances

The Aymara dance on many occasions. They dance to remember wars their people have fought. They dance to thank the gods for rain. Some of the biggest and most unusual dances are performed at festivals. In a dance called Los Llameros (the llama), performers act like herders chasing llamas on the Altiplano.

Left: Aymara dancers whirl about in their colorful costumes.

Songs to the Gods

Many Aymara songs are actually prayers. For instance, people sing the frog song to ask the gods for rain. The song is accompanied by panpipes and the croaking of frogs. How do people make the frogs croak? Maestros catch frogs from Lake Titicaca, put them in basins with some water, and leave the basins out in the sun. As the water dries up, the frogs cry out. The Aymara believe that when frogs croak, the gods will take pity on them and send rain to the Altiplano.

Below: Playing traditional instruments—such as these flutes—is still popular among the Aymara. But many Aymara teenagers are also crazy about electric guitars and drums.

THE PEÑA

The Aymara *peña* is a show of traditional Altiplano music. In rural areas, musicians often hold peñas in huts. In cities, they perform in clubs and restaurants. Besides playing music, the Aymara eat, drink, and have fun with their friends at peñas.

COLORS OF THE ALTIPLANO

The Aymara world is full of beautiful sights that have inspired artists for centuries. Traditional Aymara art mostly depicts the landscape, animals, and plants of the Altiplano. Modern Aymara art often shows the Aymara to be strong people who have survived a harsh environment and cruel rulers.

World-Famous Textiles

Aymara textiles are prized throughout the world. These textiles often show images of llamas, fish, eagles, stars, lightning bolts, and other designs. Most of the textiles are also striped, much like the patterns of the terraced mountain slopes around Lake Titicaca. The Aymara boil flowers and leaves to make dyes to color their textiles. Weavers create their works by hand, using wooden looms. Their textiles are strong and can last for many years.

Right: The patterns on Aymara textiles often represent the things they see in everyday life.

Painting the People

Some modern Aymara work as painters. One of the most famous is Mario Yllanes. His murals have been exhibited in New York and other big cities. The murals depict Aymara history and beliefs. They show the Aymara to be strong fighters. These works have inspired many Aymara people to be proud of their heritage. Mamani Mamani, who comes from Tiahuanaco, is another famous Aymara painter. He paints the beauty of his people and the Altiplano. His brightly colored paintings show the Aymara hard at work in the fields and at home.

Above: Many Aymara practice Catholicism. The painting above shows Mary and baby Jesus in front of the Puerta del Sol in the ancient city of Tiahuanaco.

Right: The Aymara weave their textiles on wooden looms and tighten the threads by hand. They might use nearly 180 threads per inch (2.5 centimeters) of cloth! This kind of weaving takes great skill and makes the cloth durable.

AYMARA HOLLYWOOD

Film is the newest art form in the Aymara community. Many Aymara have learned about filmmaking and video technology at college in the city, as well as by watching Hollywood films (*right*). Aymara filmmakers often make movies about Aymara people living within the modern world. *Chuquiago*, a Bolivian film from the 1970s, shows how the Aymara live in La Paz. Most people in the movie speak the Aymara language.

8 NOMINACIONES PARA EL OSCAR
INCLUYENDO: MEJOR PELICULA · MEJOR DIRECTOR (OLIVER STONE)
KEVIN COSTNER
CINE IMPERIAL
JFK
La Pregunta Que No Quiere Callar
HOY GRAN ESTRENO

A LASTING LANGUAGE

The Aymara language has been spoken since ancient times. In fact, the name Aymara comes from the words *jaya mara aru*, which mean "ancient language." Archaeologists aren't sure whether or not the ancient Aymara had a written language. When Spanish priests arrived in the Altiplano in the 1500s, they created a written Aymara alphabet.

Uniquely Their Own

The structure of the Aymara language is different from English. For instance, Aymara contains only three vowel sounds—*a, i,* and *u.* Some sounds in the Aymara language are not found in English at all. For example, sometimes speakers click their tongues after a *p, t, ch, k,* or *q* sound. In Aymara writing, an apostrophe after one of these letters indicates that the speaker should click his or her tongue.

Left: Although most Aymara can speak Spanish and the Aymara language, they prefer to use Aymara when talking to their families at home or on the telephone.

Borrowed Words

The modern Aymara language is not the same as the language of their ancestors. It has changed over the centuries, with many words borrowed from Spanish, including *iwisa* (sheep) and *pollera* (skirt). Aymara sounds something like the Quechua language spoken by neighboring people in the Altiplano, but the two languages have only 180 words in common.

Above: An Aymara schoolboy reading aloud—probably in the Spanish language

Using Two Languages

Spanish is the official language of Bolivia, Chile, and Peru. Most schools in these countries teach classes in Spanish, and most educated Aymara know how to speak it. The Aymara must use Spanish when they sell products in city markets. At home, however, Aymara prefer to speak their own language.

EVERYONE LOVES A STORY

And so do the Aymara. Some Aymara tales have been told for centuries. Animal tales are very common. One popular story tells how a condor and a hummingbird become human and play tricks on each other. The fox is usually a comical character in Aymara stories. When Aymara storytellers spin tales (*left*), the language comes alive.

THE SPIRITS OF NATURE

The Aymara worship the spirits of nature, including the animals, mountains, and land of the Altiplano. In their daily activities like planting potatoes, irrigating fields, and chopping eucalyptus trees for firewood, people give thanks to the spirits around them. The spirits can bring good fortune, such as plentiful harvests and lots of rainfall, or misfortune, such as bad weather. The Aymara consider the spirits to be members of the family.

Offerings to the Spirits

The Aymara religion is based on the idea of giving something each time you take something. For example, people make sacrifices and offerings to the spirits in return for blessings. Each time the Aymara plow, mine, or dig the earth, they apologize to Pachamama— Mother Earth. They pour a gift of the blood of an animal onto the ground. They sometimes sacrifice llamas dressed in silk. In return for the sacrifices, the Aymara hope that Pachamama will give them healthy crops.

Right: Aymara villagers seek blessings from Pachamama.

Folk Catholicism

Catholic priests accompanied the first Spanish rulers in the Andes. These priests converted the Aymara to Catholicism, but the Aymara did not give up their own religion entirely. Instead, they combined their traditional religion with Catholicism. The modern Aymara still practice this mix of Catholic and ancient beliefs—called folk Catholicism.

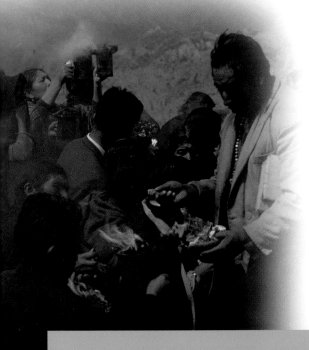

Above: Aymara women light candles in a church. The Aymara believe in Jesus, the Virgin Mary, and the saints of the Catholic religion. But they also worship the Inca Sun God and Pachamama.

ONE FOR THE ROAD

Each weekend in Copacabana, Bolivia, Aymara people decorate their cars with flowers, flags, and ribbons. They parade the cars down the street to the town's cathedral, where a priest blesses the cars (*right*). The Aymara believe that this blessing will make their vehicles safe for the drive home. Sometimes, the priest blesses whole fleets of new buses to prepare them for the mountainous Bolivian highways.

RELIGIOUS FEASTS

Feasts, or festivals, are an important part of Aymara religion and culture. Feasts often feature Catholic rituals combined with traditional Aymara dances and costumes. Many feasts include contests such as bullfights, bicycle races, and even beauty pageants.

Remembering the Dead

The Aymara believe that their ancestors pay them a visit on the first day of November. On this day, people visit cemeteries and the graves of their ancestors. They leave offerings for the dead. Sometimes, people camp overnight, telling each other stories about their dead relatives.

Below: On November 1, members of an Aymara family huddle around their ancestor's grave.

The Festival of Candelaria

The Festival of Candelaria, held each year on February 2, combines traditional and Catholic beliefs. On this day, farmers pray over their crops. They ask the gods to help the crops grow bigger. In the cities, crowds parade through the streets, carrying a doll representing the Virgin Mary. Bands of musicians follow the marchers. Some people dance in devil masks, and others wear animal costumes.

Happy Aymara New Year!

The Aymara celebrate New Year's Day on June 21. The year starts the moment the first rays of sunlight shine through the main entrance of the Kalasaya. This is a temple in Tiahuanaco where the early Aymara performed important religious rituals. The Aymara believe that the Sun God himself enters the temple along with the rays of light. He brings the spring season to the Altiplano. Buses from all over Bolivia carry crowds of people to Tiahuanaco for a predawn fiesta. The people drink, dance, and eat. But they must bundle up, because at this hour and time of year, the weather can be bitterly cold in Tiahuanaco.

Above: Dancers dress up in devil costumes on the day of the Festival of Candelaria.

AYMARA WEDDINGS

Aymara weddings (*right*) are happy occasions, typically lasting seven days. During the first six days, the families of the bride and groom, as well as other villagers, dance, eat, and drink to their fill. But the bride and groom can only sit and watch their friends and relatives have fun. They are not allowed to talk or smile. Their parents must feed them. They finally get to join in the fun on the evening of the seventh day.

RITES OF PASSAGE

Aymara children do not participate much in religious feasts. But they have celebrations of their own, full of games, fun, food, and gifts. The *kachua* is the most important children's feast. It is a rite of passage—a time when young people pass from childhood to adulthood.

Kachua Feasts

Kachuas usually take place on November 29 and December 13. Children sing and dance in groups, led by an older boy and girl, known as the *kawa iras*. Some dances are about courtship. In one dance, the boys and girls pretend not to have interest in one another. The dance is quite exciting. The participants dance fast and furiously. The girls take the lead most of the time. The boys play flutes.

Below: Aymara boys in colorful festival wear

Christmas Kachuas

At Christmastime, children hold special kachuas on hilltops close to town. The children exchange goodies. The girls give huge plates of fish, ocas, potatoes, and steamed quinoa dough to the boys. The girls try to outdo each other by offering the most food. The boys give the girls bananas, bread, pears, and sodas in return. This exchange is repeated three times. No wonder no one sings or dances very much at this feast—the partygoers are unable to move because of all they have eaten!

Above: For these schoolgirls, kachuas will mark the passage from childhood to adulthood.

The Snake Dance

At the end of Christmas kachuas, children perform the Snake Dance. They choose a new pair of kawa iras to lead the dance. The new leaders dance with dead snakes around their necks. The previous kawa iras follow them. The dancers give bread and fruit to the village maestro and ask for his blessing in return. Then the children head home to rest and digest.

THE FIRST HAIRCUT

The *rutucha* (first haircut) is another important feast for Aymara children (*right*). It takes place when a child is around two years old. Before age two, a child is considered a member of his or her family only. After the rutucha, the child becomes a member of the Aymara community at large. Only the parents and siblings of the child attend the feast. Family members present gifts to one another.

GLOSSARY

Altiplano: the high plain of southeastern Peru and western Bolivia; the Aymara homeland

altitude: height above sea level

andesite: a black volcanic rock sometimes used as a building material

archaeologist: a scientist who studies the remains of past human life and culture

colony: a group of people living in a new territory but keeping strong ties to their home country

domesticated: adapted to life with humans

haciendas (ah-SYAYN-dahs): large estates found in Spanish-speaking countries

irrigate: to bring water to crops by artificial means, using devices such as canals, pipes, and pumps

jilakata (hih-lah-KAH-tah): a male leader in an Aymara community who settles disputes and collects taxes

kachua (KAH-chwah): an Aymara rite of passage from adolescence to adulthood

kawa iras (kah-WAH ih-RAHS): a boy and a girl who lead the dances at a kachua feast

maestro (MY-stroh): a wise man or sorcerer with the power to bring rain to or send hail away from the village

mitayo (mee-TAH-yoh): a native South American miner working for the Spanish in the 1600s

nomads: people who travel from place to place, without a settled home

sacrifice: to kill an animal or person as an offering to a god

sponsor: a man who collects money during religious festivals. The money is used for community projects, such as repairing government buildings or installing new water systems.

terraces: a series of flat ridges cut into a hillside, usually to create more farmland

thresh: to separate the grains or seeds of a cereal plant by beating it

volcanoes: openings in the earth's surface through which lava, hot gases, rock fragments, and ashes periodically burst forth

FINDING OUT MORE

Books

Buechler, Hans. *The Bolivian Aymara*. New York: Holt, Rinehart, and Winston, 1971.

Clark, Ann Nolan. *Secret of the Andes*. New York: Viking Press, 1976.

Cobb, Vicki, and Barbara Lavallee. *This Place Is High: The Andes Mountains of South America*. New York: Walker and Company, 1989.

McIntyre, Loren. *The Incredible Inca and Their Timeless Land*. Washington, D.C.: National Geographic Society Press, 1975.

Parker, Edward. *Bolivia, Ecuador, Peru*. Austin, Texas: Raintree Steck-Vaughn, 1998.

Pateman, Robert. *Bolivia*. New York: Benchmark Books, 1996.

Videos

Aymara Leadership. Documentary Educational Resources, 1984.

Bolivia—Campesinos and Farming on Isla Del Sol. USDA, 1971.

Tille Qulqichaleco. Duke University, 1999.

Websites

<http://www.aymara.org>

<http://www.boliviaweb.com>

<http://www.co.multnomah.or.us/lib /homework/anchsthc.html#inca>

<http://www.nationalgeographic.com /ngm/0102/feature1/zoom1.html>

<http://www.sunspiced.com /phistory.html>

Organizations

Center for World Indigenous Studies
PMB 214
1001 Cooper Point Road S.W., Suite 140
Olympia, WA 98502-1107 USA
360/754-1990
Website: <http://www.cwis.org>

The Indigenous Language Institute
560 Montezuma Avenue
Santa Fe, NM 87501
505/820-0311
Website: <http://www.ipola.org /index.html>

INDEX

ABOUT THE AUTHOR

James Eagen is a writer and a teacher. He holds a graduate degree in international and comparative education from Columbia University. He has served as the middle school head of an international school in New York City and has taught in numerous other places, including Prague in the Czech Republic and Santa Fe, New Mexico. James has also traveled around South America, spending time with the Indian people of the Andes. He currently lives in Ithaca, New York.